101

REASONS TO VOTE

AGAINST

HILLARY

101

REASONS TO VOTE

AGAINST

HILLARY

WILSON CASEY

Skyhorse Publishing

Skyhorse Publishing books may be purchased in bulk at special discounts for sales promotion, corporate gifts, fund-raising, or educational purposes. Special editions can also be created to specifications. For details, contact the Special Sales Department, Skyhorse Publishing, 307 West 36th Street, 11th Floor, New York, NY 10018 or info@skyhorsepublishing.com.

Skyhorse® and Skyhorse Publishing® are registered trademarks of Skyhorse Publishing, Inc.®, a Delaware corporation.

Visit our website at www.skyhorsepublishing.com.

10 9 8 7 6 5 4 3 2 1

Library of Congress Cataloging-in-Publication Data is available on file.

Cover design by Rain Saukas
Cover photo credit: AP Images
Interior photos: iStock and Shutterstock

ISBN: 978-1-63450-579-6
Ebook ISBN: 978-1-63450-636-6

Printed in the United States of America

Dedication

To my daughter, Colleen Adaire Casey, the possessor of great fortitude—you are my heart.

INTRODUCTION

Hillary Clinton—you're either *for* her or you are *against* her. And if you're against her, you'll find an ample stockpile of reasons in this book to help you convince your friends, family, coworkers, and even complete strangers of why they should be, too. It's important that you're involved because Hillary is on a trajectory that might make her the most powerful person in the world for the next four years! Even Senator Lindsey Graham, who ran for a while in the Republican primaries, who doesn't like Hillary, who calls her the most dishonest person in America . . . even he thinks that she'll be the next president of the United States if she runs against Donald Trump. So this election matters. And if you care, you should read my books.

By trade I'm a syndicated columnist, multi-published author, professional speaker, and "Trivia Guy" with Guinness World Record–holding credentials, but there's nothing *trivial* when it comes to deciding the next president of the United States. Your decision of whom to vote for in the 2016 campaign puts you in the *personal* mix for the future of yourself, your family, friends, and, most importantly, for America.

In trying to find the slippery and fragmented truth in this complicated political landscape, you have to blend public pronouncements and media coverage with personal feelings. It's hard to speak softly, to think before you shout. Normally I'm not one to orate on national politics from the top of Mount Pundit, but when you write about politics, you're forced to raise your voice. And it also helps to have a sense of humor.

Politics is big business. Most politicians acknowledge that, at least privately. And like all businesses, politics has specific rules of the roads, paths, and processes. These affect how candidates are perceived and elected, who gets into office, or who falls by the wayside. So if one aims to be the next president of the United States, she not only needs to be a great speaker and motivator, but an expert on how the political system works and how this affects voter choices. No one understands those key points better than Hillary Clinton.

All her angles, aspects, and strategies are covered. She not only plays the game, but she's the referee and also the fan in the stands. She's *that* good at what she does best—being a longtime successful politician in the limelight. She's a rabble rouser and crowd pleaser with whomever she's in front of. There's *no* denying that.

All voters make decisions, but so many make choices based on things as trivial as a candidate's untimely smirk, or sweat in front of a camera, or hairdo, or clothes. Elections aren't just about voting for someone. It's equally valid and in fact your duty to vote **against** a candidate if you feel she is absolutely the worst possible choice to be president. Many voters form their opinions on national political figures for purely personal or outrageously partisan reasons. That *seems* to be human nature.

Here in these pages I've given you 101 solid reasons to vote against her. They are not listed in any order of priority. The 1–101 numbering simply helps as reference points. Whatever your feelings toward Hillary Clinton, these reasons will better prepare you to participate in the upcoming battle to choose the next president of the United States of America.

Your opinion and vote *truly* matter.

Wilson Casey
Spartanburg, SC
TriviaGuy.com

P.S. For the well-rounded picture, be sure to check out my other work, ***101 Reasons to Vote for Hillary***, covering the other side of Hillary Clinton's political coin. Thanks, and happy voting!

101

REASONS TO VOTE

AGAINST

HILLARY

1. She's married to Bill. Seriously, do you need any more reasons than that? His nickname is "Slick Willy." He's one of only two US presidents ever to be impeached. He looked the American people in the eye and lied. And what did Hillary do? She stood by her man.

2. Does anyone want a third term for Obama? President Hillary Clinton would be just that if she wins. Obamacare would be here to stay, more government spending designed to punish small business while coddling the poor, and a foreign policy so weak and misguided that America's allies don't know if they can trust us anymore, and America's enemies don't fear us.

3. Hillary spent four years as secretary of state, a plum assignment that came her way in what seems to have been a thank you from Obama for supporting him in the general election. Will her name rank up there with Thomas Jefferson, John Quincy Adams, Henry Kissinger, and James Baker? What did she accomplish in four years? Benghazi.

4. Her tenure as a senator from New York was from January 2001 to January 2009. During those years only three bills she sponsored became law. Only three! They were uncontroversial matters that passed by unanimous consent in the Senate and voice vote in the House. The question that needs to be addressed: isn't a lawmaker supposed to pass bills? It's certainly true that buddy-buddy senators customarily have their names listed as many times as possible as cosponsors of bills. Hillary Clinton had her name as sponsor on three laws in eight years with not a single piece of landmark legislation. Some accomplishments!

5. Now she's a diehard Democrat, but as a young woman she was active in Republican groups and campaigned for Republican presidential nominee Barry Goldwater in 1964. Her flip-flopping tendencies have carried over into the remainder of her political life, especially on the border crisis regarding innocent immigrant children. She cosponsored The Dream Act that would allow the children of illegal immigrants to earn legal status in this country if they pursue a college education or enlist in the military. Earlier, she was adamantly against illegal immigrants and now is promising to push for citizenship for those in the country illegally. More of this same continual flip-flopping on issues is to be expected if she becomes president.

6. What's her main qualification? That's she's smarter? That's she's tougher? That she is better able to keep America safe? No. Her number one qualification seems to be that she's a woman. We've had eight years of another president who was a first, and look what that got us. We don't need more affirmative action. We need conservative action.

7. She turns sixty-nine years old on October 26, 2016. She'd be just months younger than our oldest president, Ronald Reagan, when he was elected in 1980. As great as Reagan was, he was slipping toward the end of his second term. Would Hillary be physically up to the challenge? It's doubtful. The most exercise she gets is wagging her chin and finger.

8. Years ago, when we had a Republican in the White House, we had Steve **Jobs**, Bob **Hope**, and Johnny **Cash**. Today we have no *jobs*, no *hope*, and no *cash*. Diapers and Democrats should be changed often—both for the same reason. Hillary Clinton is endorsed by Barack Obama. Perhaps enough said. That's a very good reason not to vote for her, but let's clarify. Given Obama's track record, he may not have meant she was an excellent choice. Simply ask a cross-section of your friends if they like the direction the country is headed in and if they feel better off now than they were eight years ago. Many will say "no." If you want some serious "hope and change," can you or your friends vote for more of the same? I don't think so.

9.   Even her airport sucks! A 2013 survey of travelers to Clinton National Airport in Little Rock, Arkansas, rated it as the worst of the sixty-seven domestic airports considered in the survey. Democrats and Republicans alike have griped about the airport's long security lines, poor check-ins, bad designs, little food availability, and terrible shopping. It seems Hillary Clinton would have made a few calls to help out, especially regarding something with her name on it.

10. Hillary Clinton is terrified about religion "worming its way" into government. When she was asked about the Supreme Court's 2014 ruling on the Hobby Lobby and Conestoga corporations, she replied, "I disagree with the reasoning as well as the conclusion." The decision concerned the companies' sincerely held religious beliefs in that they did not have to provide a full range of contraceptives at no cost to employees. Clinton explained. "It is a disturbing trend that you see in a lot of societies that are unstable and prone to extremism." She went on to say that something similar was happening in the United States.

11. She has won votes in the primaries, but she hasn't won hearts. Most Americans still don't like her. Historians and political analysts are struggling to find an era when more than half the country has held such stubbornly low opinions of the presidential hopeful in the Democratic Party. Although Mrs. Clinton is viewed as a more seasoned political figurehead, her campaign has lagged to win the trust of the American electorate. There's nothing fresh about her. If she's elected, trends certainly dictate there'd be more scandals and power abuse of all types from the Clinton camp.

12. Hillary Clinton voted for the War in Iraq and for the un-American Patriot Act *twice* despite the fact that it damaged American liberty without protecting the country. Don't vote for Hillary if you don't like war, as the president of the United States has the power to unilaterally wage war. On NBC's *Meet the Press* Senator Rand Paul said, "We're worried that Hillary Clinton will get us involved in another Middle Eastern war, because she's so gung-ho." Clinton's foreign policy is more hawkish than Trump's, and unlike Trump, she has a record to prove it. As a senator in 2002 Hillary Clinton voted in favor of providing President George W. Bush the broad authority to invade Iraq.

13. Insiders and White House staffers spoke very candidly with Ronald Kessler, author of a 2014 book revealing the hidden lives of the first family during the Bill Clinton presidency. One insider was quoted, "Hillary is woefully disorganized and habitually late." Author Kessler notes that showing up on time won't be a feature of a Hillary Clinton presidency. Another staffer said (referring to earlier elections), "She had children running her campaign. She had a lack of organization and a lack of maturity. She could not keep a schedule." Kessler's work lays out time after time of rude, insolent, belligerent behavior by Hillary Clinton. That clearly demonstrates she is unfit to represent the United States and more reason she is undeserving of the presidency.

14. Does anyone really believe Hillary should be the first woman to be president? Think of all the women who should come before her. We have women CEOs, generals, scientists, and even politicians who have all done more and done it honestly in service of their country than Hillary.

15. Hillary Clinton, Commander-in-Chief. Did you feel a shiver go up your spine? It's a scary thought. She has absolutely no experience in the military, and when she convinced the Obama administration to overthrow the regime in Libya, she made a complete and utter mess of it.

16. Young women as a group do not support Hillary. It's neither sexism making them flee, nor Hillary being in her late sixties. It's that she's out of touch with what women want in America. So what's the drive to elect the first female president when women in America don't want her?

17. Hillary Clinton has too many skeletons in the closet, figuratively and literally. Mary Mohane, former White House intern, was expected to testify about sexual harassment at the White House. She was gunned down in a coffee shop. Nothing was taken. Vincent Foster, former White House counsel, who had significant knowledge of the Clintons' financial affairs and was a business partner with Hillary, he was found dead of a gunshot wound to the head that was ruled a suicide.

18. And then there's C. Victor Raiser, II, former national finance co-chairman of Clinton for President, and Montgomery Raiser, his son. They both perished in a suspicious plane crash in Alaska. Paul Tully, DNC political director, was a key member of the damage control squad and Clinton strategist. He was found dead in a Little Rock hotel room with no cause ever determined, nor was an autopsy allowed.

19. It gets worse. Ed Willey, a major Clinton fund raiser, was found with a gunshot wound to the head in the woods of Virginia. It was ruled a suicide. His wife went public about a Clinton groping incident. Jerry Parks, a former security team member for Governor Clinton, had compiled an extensive file on Clinton activities. His family had reported to authorities of being followed. His home was broken into shortly before he was gunned down at a deserted intersection.

20. Sadly, the list goes on. John Wilson, a former Washington, DC Council member who had ties to Whitewater, he perished of a very suspicious hanging suicide. Dr. Donald Rogers, a dentist who was killed in a suspicious plane crash on his way to an interview with a reporter to reveal information about Clinton. Can they all be coincidences?

21. She's all about NAFTA (North American Free Trade Agreement) and CAFTA (Central America Free Trade Agreement), and giving us the SHAFTA. NAFTA is a 1994 treaty made among the United States, Canada, and Mexico with its negatives of environmental and employment issues. 2004's CAFTA expanded the failed NAFTA model. Hillary once sat on Walmart's board of directors and oversaw the changes that led to the massive influx of cheap, economy-destroying Chinese goods.

:

22. She's burnt out on politics. She's been a lifer in that profession. America doesn't want to go through the motions of electing a life-long politician that feels entitled to another promotion, this time to the highest office in the land. Hillary has a "Washington-knows-best" mentality, and she's a "Creature of Washington."

23. Her fees for speaking engagements are out the wazoo—$675,000 for three speeches to Goldman Sachs—and although she denies it, it's hard to believe that such sums won't influence her decisions. Hillary Clinton, with all her rich friends, has raised and is continuing to raise a lot of money. Sadly, it is being used to slam her opponents instead of running a positive campaign. She slammed Bernie Sanders, and she'll slam the Republican candidate when the primaries are over.

24. Does America really want H I L L A R Y as President of the United States? The letters could represent: Hateful, Idealistic, Lying, Liberal, Arse, Ruling, You.

25. This time around the Republicans have someone to vote for! A big problem in the past two campaigns was that people were more interested in voting *against* Obama than either *for* Romney or McCain. The 2016 Republican candidate, Donald Trump, is giving hope to millions of Americans who are fed up and forgotten by the Washington elites.

26. Retire her! She's had an unnoteworthy political career already. Why send her to the White House? Her arguments to be a good president have been too complicated and un-inspired for the people out there to grasp. Her expectation to win just by announcement is insulting and too cocky. There's no "hope" or "change" as sound logic in Hillary Clinton's campaign.

27. The middle class is getting screwed by the current administration's domestic agenda—wages are stagnant and inflation is beginning to creep up—and there would be more of the same with Hillary. The US labor market has lost much of its power to deliver a living wage. The real nature of America's problem is not a lack of Hillary ideas about how to improve the lives of workers. It is the lack of political will to put them in practice. Success doesn't hinge on a list of proposals. It will require reshaping entrenched political Democratic Party positions. That is something Hillary Clinton will never have the will to do. Relying on corporate incentives to change the economics and hope of the middle class is irretrievably naïve.

28. Her highly publicized book *Hard Choices* was nothing more than a campaign promotion focusing on foreign affairs. Her reviews were much more bad than good. One reviewer said it was good for constipation, as he had been backed up for a long time with Democratic Pooty. This book was written with the sure knowledge that it would be dissected, not read. The amount she paid loyalists to help her write it destined the work to be purchased and not looked at, a volume given but not opened. Hillary's political memoirs is a disappointing genre. *Hard Choices* is a $35 book that's overhyped. The same holds true for Hillary Clinton.

29. Supporters of Hillary Clinton have the impossible task of defending her against countless numbers of high-profile scandals. Hillary is a cunning lawyer who knows how to point blame away from her camp. From Whitewater to Travelgate to Filegate to Benghazi. And those are just the ones publicized. Let's take Whitewater, for example. No normal law-abiding person would have been able to arrange for the investment in Whitewater properties located in the Ozark Mountains (Arkansas) or get away with taking massive tax write-offs that were illegal from the losses later assumed. It was an orchestrated crime scheme by the Clintons in which their business partner, developer Jim McDougal, died while serving a sentence for his part. And yet, no deserved jail time for Hillary or Bill.

30. In the press she commented about the Clintons being "dead broke" when they left the White House in 2001, and later conceded that comment was "inartful." (The word *inartful* is not in most dictionaries, but as a politician she's allowed to make up words as needed. We think this one is a synonym for "lie.") She later told ABC news that all of the money she's made from colleges ($220,000 in speaking engagements) since she left her post as secretary of state has been donated to a nonprofit foundation—hers.

31. Hillary Clinton had a moment on TV's *Meet the Press* (April 3, 2016) when she was talking about abortion and referred to an "unborn person." That term is not typically used by people who support legal abortion. In fact, the *New York Times* put out a headline: "Hillary Clinton Roundly Criticized for Referring to the Unborn as a 'Person.'" Dehumanizing language is an important key to supporters of the abortion industry who proclaim that defining fetuses as "persons" should mean they are entitled to a right to life under the 14th Amendment, something they desperately want to keep from happening. Hillary is pro-choice but consistently uses the Democratic Party rhetoric that abortion should be "safe, legal, and rare." That stand makes her transparent and taking a "poll-tested path" to please voters. If she's suggesting that it's okay to abort up until birth, she's greatly out of line with the American people and most states' current laws.

32. With Republicans in charge of the House and Senate, we have a Republican-leaning political landscape. Hillary Clinton should not be considered the favorite no matter what the media-controlled polls may say, so don't waste a vote on her. She's no more than a generic Democratic candidate.

33. She treated Benghazi 2012 as a public relations matter to massage, instead of the murder of our ambassador and others. The sovereignty of the United States was discounted as worthless when she said at a congressional hearing, "What difference does it make what we knew and when we knew it?" Hillary Clinton refused to hand over Benghazi notes. Is a government cover-up the best way to persuade people of her innocence in the matter?

34. She was a key figure in pushing health care reform that was the pre-cursor to Obamacare. The Republican National Committee has said that Mrs. Clinton's health care proposals were "a tacit admission that the president's health law hasn't succeeded." Republican spokesperson Michael Short proclaimed, "Doubling down on the same principles is only a recipe for more failure. Rather than putting the federal government in even more control, Hillary Clinton should focus on market-based reforms that would actually lower costs and expand access."

35. Hillary Clinton lied about being shot at in Bosnia in 1996, but whereas NBC news anchor Brian Williams was widely criticized for claiming that he was on a helicopter that was shot down in Iraq in 2003, Clinton got a pass for her lie. This woman hasn't told the truth since she learned how to talk.

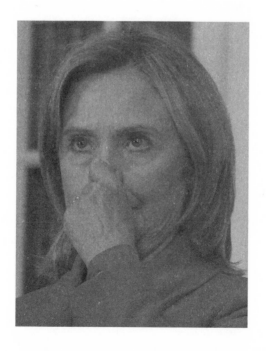

36. The 2014 midterm election results across the board were enough to prove the momentum is on the Republican side. Voters are tired and afraid of what could be a possible Clinton monarchy. Sweeping gains were attained by the Republican Party in the Senate, House, and in numerous gubernatorial, state, and local races. On gaining control of the Senate for the first time since 2006, the Republicans also increased their majority in the House. They also gained two seats in governors' races. Senator Rand Paul, Republican-Kentucky, tweeted on a personal reference to Hillary, "You didn't think it could get worse than your book tour? It did. Courtesy of the U.S. voters."

37. Hillary Clinton is already attracting unwanted attention about her funding from large banks, such as Citigroup, Goldman Sachs, J. P. Morgan Chase, and Morgan Stanley. It'd be nice if Hillary Clinton would dress like a NASCAR driver so we could easily identify her corporate sponsors.

38. She doesn't have a core message. Her husband, Bill, has even said, "We've reached a point in our life when we think you really shouldn't run for office if you don't have a clear idea of what you can do, and a unique contribution you can make and you can outline that. I think so much of politics is background noise, and we don't need the background noise anymore."

39. Is the 2.0 version (2016) really any better than the 1.0 version (2008)? She is who she is and cannot change. The 2.0 version has more bugs, snags, and problems than the 1.0. Shouldn't it be the other way around? Shouldn't the kinks have been ironed out? The late-breaking downturn in Hillary Clinton's 2016 campaign is more unexpected than in 2008. Her national polling lead, which has been holding steady for months, has plummeted faster than it did eight years ago The drop has been with less warning, and her camp's advisors don't know why. Her current 2016 campaign (2.0 version) should be easer than her first (1.0 version) in 2008. It isn't.

40. Hillary has been adamantly against the efforts by some to make English the official language of the United States of America. So what language is her choice? She doesn't say, but does she think we should not be, in any way, discriminating against people who do not speak English. Fair enough, but to paraphrase a John Wayne movie character, "If you're good enough to come to our country, you better be good enough to learn our language."

41. By her own account, we are now second-fiddle in key areas to our neighbor to the north, Canada. How can the U.S. be an economic super power if it's not number one on its own continent? In a speech she said, "Canadian middle-class incomes are now higher than in the United States. They are working fewer hours for more pay, enjoying a stronger safety net, living longer on average, and facing less income inequality." This happened on Obama's watch. She'll wear the same watch.

42. Her delays in officially announcing until Sunday, April 12, 2015, showed even she isn't sure if she wants the job. The American public is tired of the same old people showing up to run for office. Bernie Sanders proudly calls himself a Democratic Socialist, and in the primaries he has pulled Hillary in that direction because she doesn't have a solid core of what kind of leader to be, just that she wants power.

43. Chicago Cub fans are in every state in the nation. They are loyal and always pull for their team. Hillary Clinton was born and raised in Illinois and billed herself as a Cubs fan. She has forsaken them. She has sold them out. During her Senate campaign she changed to become a New York Yankees fan just to get more votes. Hillary Clinton cries when it's politically helpful. She acts tough when politically helpful, and she acts graceful when politically helpful.

44. When Clinton met Sir Edmond Hillary in 1995, she claimed her mother named her Hillary and with two "l's" after him. The only problem, he didn't make news climbing anything until almost six years after Hillary Rodham was born. It's just another example of Hillary Clinton stretching the truth to suit her agenda.

45. Those who are unemployed want jobs. Those who have jobs want pay raises. All that most will remember are eight lean years under Barack Obama. How can they be better off with another Democrat in the White House? The backbone of America is average people fighting to survive. Hillary Clinton's main money and backers come from Wall Street and Silicon Valley. For example, Sheryl Sandberg, the CFO of Facebook, supports her, as does Marc Benioff, the CEO of Salesforce. She doesn't represent middle-class people.

46. Hillary Clinton has no clarity of thought, nor direct plans of action to thwart threats posed by radical terrorism. Senator Ted Cruz of Texas said it best: "Leading from behind doesn't work." He's also said the threats facing us today are "every bit as ominous" as those faced before World War II.

47. If you hear "Ready for Hillary," honestly ask yourself, "Ready for what?" More of the Democrap? To name a few, she'll have to run from Bill's record. She'll have to run from Obama's record. She'll have to run from Benghazigate. She'll have to run from more sniper fire. She won't have any time to campaign for all the running! Her new slogan is, "Don't believe the lies I told you then, believe the ones I tell you now!"

48. From law school gobbledygook: When the law is against you, argue the facts. When the facts are against you, argue the law. When both are against you, pound the podium. Hillary Clinton certainly pounds the podium with her campaign promises, jargon, and one-liners. But as we all know, talk is cheap. She'll say anything to attract voters, but there's rarely a definite plan of action.

49. Clinton did not have a governmental email address during her tenure as secretary of state. She blatantly ignored federal guidelines and used her own private email to conduct business on behalf of the United States of America. She didn't play by the same rules as everybody else in Washington, DC. She knows no boundaries, and the email scandal is just another example from a long list where she always lawyers herself up.

50. Hillary Clinton brags about her nearly one million miles traveled for America's interests during her four years as secretary of state. During that globetrotting tenure, she set the record as the most well-traveled U.S. envoy in history. A former Hewlett-Packard CEO rebutted that she, too, had traveled many hundreds of thousands of miles around the globe, but had actually accomplished something. The exec said, "You see, Mrs. Clinton, flying is not an accomplishment, it is an activity."

51. From a Starbucks metaphor: do voters want something "fresh" or something "old" that's been around? When you go in after 2 p.m., you can get a morning bun for a buck. The price goes down after something has been around too long. Hillary Clinton is like that old bun in the afternoon. It's time for some fresh pastry in the White House. Vote Republican!

52. Please ask yourself some serious questions. Was Hillary Clinton's tenure as secretary of state a success? A resounding no! Was she naïve about Russia's aggressiveness? A resounding yes! Hillary Clinton says her relationship with Russian President Putin is "interesting." Does she have real answers to the economic health of the middle class? A resounding no! Can she protect our foreign interests when she couldn't even protect diplomats in Benghazi? A resounding no! Should you or anyone vote for her? A resounding no!

53. The Democratic party has real challenges in 2016 and will have even more down the road. They've lost a number of gubernatorial races in 2010 and 2014. Their losses also extend down to the local levels. That means there are fewer future candidates in the pipeline. Hillary Clinton can't be a good queen bee without worker ants.

54. Nobody likes to be talked down to. That is exactly what Hillary Clinton did when she weighed in on the children's vaccine debate in her tweet, "The science is clear: The earth is round, the sky is blue, and #vaccineswork. Let's protect all our kids. #GrandmothersKnowBest." Although many agree with its protecting message, many don't like her inflated ego.

55. Though the Democrats won't publically admit it, they all want Hillary as president and Bill as vice president. Bill would be the unofficial VP no matter who's designated the vice presidential candidate. Heaven save us if Hillary's elected.

56. While Hillary Clinton seems to have become a celebrity politician and is presumably loved and admired by many, she sidesteps issues. She plays it safe instead of trying to be a leader. Her past accomplishments so far have been quite meager. It is definitely not clear if she will be able to do any better as president. There are no valid reasons to vote for her. The high school mentality of thinking the presidential race is a popularity contest is not grounds to put her in the White House.

57. They say the unemployed book-signer Hillary Clinton is even more popular than Barack Obama. The reason is she has been insulated from accountability. All that will change if she's elected president and takes up right where Obama left off. She'll receive the same scrutiny and criticism as Obama, and the country will continue to flounder.

58. The Democratic party waited until deep in the game to put their starting quarterback in. They did that to protect her, but as one Hillary Clinton supporter warned, "The American people don't like to see a candidate assume that something is theirs for the taking." The Democratic party's plan backfired, and Bernie Sanders has been a tougher-than-expected opponent. He's especially popular among young people. What does it say about Hillary that young Democrats prefer an old man with wild ideas?

59. On C-SPAN a few years back (June 21, 2004), Hillary Clinton said, "I wonder if it's possible to be a Republican and a Christian at the same time." That comment is extremely offensive not only to Republicans with Christian beliefs, but also to Democrats with Christian beliefs. It's rude to all Christians.

60. In the US Senate elections of 2014, almost every candidate Hillary campaigned for lost, including Georgia's Michelle Nunn, Iowa's Bruce Braley, North Carolina's Kay Hagan, and Kentucky's Alison Lundergan Grimes. The Hillary Democrats got wiped out. Republican Rand Paul explained it: "Clearly, Hillary is yesterday's news." That year, with a total net increase of nine seats, the Republicans made the largest US Senate gain by any party since 1980.

61. Charlotte Clinton Mezvinsky has been dubbed "The Clinton baby." She has three grandparents who were in Congress. Two of those three have criminal records to highlight: Bill Clinton was impeached as president; Ed Mezvinsky pleaded guilty to swindling more than $10 million.

62. Even if now and then Hillary seems to be leading in all the polls, don't let them become a self-fulfilling prophecy. The election isn't until November. Also, a statistics professor at Columbia University stated, "All these media organizations are using pretty much the same information, so it is no surprise that their predictions are similar." They could all be wrong.

63. Hillary Clinton says she's in favor of transparency, but she likes to keep secrets. A Los Angeles writer, Carl Anthony, who has interviewed Mrs. Clinton and written extensively about first ladies, stated, "She explicitly told me she didn't put a lot in writing because everything in writing, including a personal diary, could be subpoenaed."

64. The Mayor of London, Boris Johnson, is on record (2007 article, *The Daily Telegraph*) as saying, "[Hillary has] everything I came into politics to oppose [including] an all-round purse-lipped political correctness." She's not a visionary. She relies too much on Bill Clinton's and Barack Obama's old political advisors, such as Jennifer Palmieri, Jim Margolis, and Joel Benenson. Johnson also compared Hillary Clinton to "a sadistic nurse in a mental hospital." He later apologized.

65. The facts remain: North Korea is ruled by its third Kim, Syria by its second Assad, and Cuba by its second Castro. We had a second Bush, and that didn't work well. We definitely don't want a second Clinton. The second go-round doesn't work in any country or regime. New ideas and new philosophies are needed. Albert Einstein's definition of insanity: "Doing the same thing over and over again and expecting different results." Electing Hillary Clinton as president and expecting the country to be better is insane.

66. Although Hillary stood by Bill throughout the Monica Lewinsky scandal, and others, she claimed on *60 Minutes* that she was not "some little woman standing by her man like Tammy Wynette." What's the difference? *New York Times* columnist William Safire said in 1996, after looking into the Starr investigation of Bill and Hillary, that the first lady was "a congenital liar."

67. When the progressive candidate Bernie Sanders began to gain momentum in the Democratic primaries, Hillary Clinton, who has always been a moderate Democrat, felt the heat and began to claim, "I'm a progressive." She makes things up. She said, "We now have more jobs in solar than we do in oil." We don't.

68. Hillary Clinton said, ISIS is "going to people showing videos of Donald Trump insulting Islam and Muslims in order to recruit more radical jihadists," but there's no evidence of that.

69. She said that hedge fund managers "pay less in taxes than nurses and truck drivers." No. For some of them the percentage of their income tax is lower, but the net tax paid is much larger, so the claim is very misleading.

70. The book *Clinton Cash: How and Why Foreign Governments and Businesses Help Make Bill and Hillary Rich* (to be released in May 2016), claims that Hillary changed her position on restrictions on India's nuclear weapons after her enterprises received big donations from India. Hillary Clinton firmly supported President Obama's nuclear arms deal with Iran, which made many concessions to that country.

71. Bill Clinton has said that his wife worked on "legal services for the poor" in law school, but according to Dick Morris, a former advisor to the Clintons who has become highly critical of them, her principal activity in law school was to work for the Black Panthers, a revolutionary black nationalist and socialist organization active in the United States from 1966 until 1982.

72. Several investigations, most notably by Representative Trey Gowdy, who, by the way, is from the same town as the writer of this work (Spartanburg, SC), continue into her exclusive use of a nongovernment email account and homebrew server while she was in government, an issue that has persisted in her presidential campaign. At the very least, it sheds light on a management style she undoubtedly would take with her to the White House. The revelation is that she has no serious regards on national security protocols in correspondences between herself and advisors, friends, and political acquaintances.

73. Come November 2016, once voters are staring down the barrel of a possible Hillary Clinton presidency, most will come to their senses and not vote for her. The possibility of additional years of the United States' soft borders and failure to fight global jihad, plus her flagrant and consistent abuse of power, is frightening. It's time for a cleansing rebirth from the sorry status quo of the Democratic Party. Donald Trump's "Make America Great Again" is a valid slogan, as a changing of the Democratic guard is certainly warranted.

74. Fox News Channel's *Outnumbered* host Andrea Tantaros says, "Anyone who sees '13 Hours' and still votes for Clinton is a criminal." Tantaros was referring to Michael Bay's movie that chronicled what happened during the Benghazi attack. She said that Hillary Clinton is lucky that Michael Bay really didn't go further with that moviemaking in that it really points to credibility. Tantaros further added she would take the word of the actual men who survived the Benghazi attack over Clinton's word any day. No matter how you slice it, critics have questioned why the world's greatest military force could not get to Benghazi (September 11, 2012) in time to defend our people. The tragedy occurred on Hillary Clinton's watch as secretary of state.

75. At an October 2015, town hall–style campaign event in Iowa, she said, "Probably one of the most egregious, wrong, pieces of legislation that ever passed the Congress when it comes to this issue is to protect gun sellers and gun makers from liability. They are the only business in America that is wholly protected from any kind of liability. They can sell a gun to someone they know they shouldn't, and they won't be sued. There will be no consequences." Hillary Clinton was wrong in her statements, as the gun industry is susceptible to some lawsuits, and there are federal laws restricting liability for numerous other types of businesses.

76. In an August 2015 tweet Hillary Clinton said, "Not one of the 17 GOP candidates has discussed how they'd address the rising cost of college." That was a totally false statement, a horrific lie. While Marco Rubio and Chris Christie laid out several specific plans for reforming postsecondary education with an eye reining in costs, practically all the GOP candidates had some form of plan. Carly Fiorina, the former technology executive, said in July 2015 that student debt was out of control because "the federal government under Democrats has nationalized the student loan business."

77. Whopper-telling alert! In April 2015 in Iowa while speaking at a business round-table inside a produce store, Hillary Clinton claimed, "All my grandparents came to the U.S. from foreign countries." It was simply a politician's flubbing of her family's ancestry while making the case to get votes, as she related her personal heritage to the struggles of undocumented immigrants trying to work in the United States. The facts: Clinton's paternal grandfather, Hugh Rodham Sr., was born in England, but her three other grandparents were born in the good ole USA.

78. During one of the Democratic debates (January 2016) she used lawyer-like tactics intending to skirt criticism about Wall Street probes from her opponents, especially on outlandish speaking fees and appearances. Bernie Sanders told her, "I don't get personal speaking fees from Goldman Sachs," noting that Ms. Clinton received $600,000 from Goldman Sachs in one year alone. Hillary's reaction diverged into meaningless rhetoric. The facts show that eight financial firms, including Goldman Sachs and Citigroup have paid Hillary and Bill Clinton between $1.6 and $3.5 million combined in speech fees.

79. Would you still support her if she were a man? Let's pretend Hillary is now "Henry." Would you be excited about *his* programs, policies, and career achievements? If you say NO, you're only supporting Hillary because of gender, which is pretty stupid. The presidency should not be about filling a quota or thinking you'd like to be a part of making herstory . . . er . . . history. Are you a woman? Yes or no? If yes, congratulations! You've just met my criteria for being president of the United States. *Not!*

80. It's noteworthy that many secular Americans would find some of the company she keeps disturbing. Beginning in 1993, Clinton was a member of "The Fellowship," a clandestine and influential evangelical group that many consider a cult. Through the years it has recruited many prominent figures in business and politics and holds meetings in gender-segregated "cells." The Fellowship's leadership includes Douglas Coe who is often referred to as the "stealth Billy Graham." The Fellowship is shrouded in mystery, but continues to manage and influence many behind-the-scenes governmental and legal policies. Its headquarters are in Washington, DC, in a mansion known as "The Cedars," with its core members calling themselves the new chosen.

81. She actually did say a Karl Marx–like, "We're going to take things away from you on behalf of the common good." Although it was spoken in 2004, it's certainly not something a presidential hopeful should ever say or think in any context. The statement was addressed to well-to-do Democrats attending a fund-raiser for California Senator Barbara Boxer. Clinton's statement probably referred to a desire to repeal tax cuts enacted by the Bush administration, which Democrats had criticized as favoring the wealthy. Still, Americans don't like hearing Communist-like debacles.

82. Voting for the lesser of two evils will still only get you evil. If you're possibly thinking to only vote for Hillary as she's the lesser of two evils, don't do it. The lesser of two evils is also referred to as a "necessary evil." It's the principle that when faced with selecting from two unpleasant options, the one that is least harmful should be chosen. This scenario is commonly known as the no-win situation referring to an unavoidable decision between two tough choices. Hillary Clinton is not the less evil. She's the more evil. "Vote for the hair, not the witch's lair."

83. Hillary Clinton is *not* a champion of the middle class. Despite trying to present herself as such, she is definitely not just like you and me. She is married to a former president, is a former senator, a former secretary of state, has a personal chef, a personal physician, a personal jet, countless other personal perks, and makes around $200,000 per speaking engagement. So that's you, right? Possibly so, but doubtful. And your middle-class neighbors—they let you use their private jet parked out back anytime you need it, right? America's not ready for Hillary, nor will they ever be. But we are ready to take our country back.

84. While some get up every day to do good, Hillary Clinton gets up every day to do bad. It goes back to her being a full partner with her husband in unethical conduct during the presidency of Bill Clinton. It's hard to forget "Pardongate" at the very end of the Clinton presidency when there were a series of questionable presidential pardons. Among the rogues gallery were four convicted swindlers from New Square, New York. A *New York Times* columnist, Bob Herbert, wrote, "You can't lead a nation if you are ashamed of the leadership of your party. The Clintons are a terminally unethical and vulgar couple, and they've betrayed everyone who has ever believed in them."

85. The Obama White House called most of the shots when Hillary Clinton was secretary of state, but as a *Wall Street Journal* columnist put it, to the status of "the least consequential secretary of state since William Rogers warmed the seat in the early years of the Nixon administration." Hillary Clinton, at a minimum, was the one who poorly executed disastrous strategies time and again. One of many examples was when she presided over appeasing policies that encouraged Vladimir Putin to protrude on his territorial and strategic ambitions (Ukraine and others). Clinton delivered a misnamed "reset" button to the Russians.

86. I've always believed that you can find a poll to believe anything you want to believe about any and every thing; the same holds true for surveys. What amazed me in the Democratic primaries was that Bernie Sanders polled better against the Republicans than did Hillary Clinton. How did a self-declared socialist (Sanders) do better than a capitalist (Hillary) to the core? The answer was simple. Bernie was everything Hillary is not. The same holds true for The Donald. He doesn't first need to test his lines in some focus group. You know exactly from where he's coming from. Agree or disagree, you know exactly his thoughts. With Hillary, it's spin after spin after spin to suit her agenda. That doesn't fare well with voters. The plain and simple truth is that Hillary is a much bigger risk than The Donald.

87. Clinton supports the closing of the Guantanamo Bay detention facility in Cuba, as it's a continuing recruitment advertisement for terrorists. So be it. If you commit an act of terror against the United States, you're going to Guantanamo. Isn't that a deterrent? Donald Trump certainly thinks so. He wants to keep Guantanamo open and fill it with more terrorists. What Trump doesn't understand is why it costs so much to maintain this place. He says, "I would guarantee you that I could do it for a tiny fraction ... maybe like peanuts. Maybe in our deal with Cuba we'll get them to take it over and reimburse us because we're probably paying rent." Like Obama, Hillary wants to close GITMO and move the terrorists to jails *inside* the United States.

88. The mainstream media have been fond of saying Mrs. Clinton is not the "subject" of any FBI investigation regarding any questionable wrongdoings on any matter. The allusion is there per a technical matter. The FBI may be poking around on its own, but no one can be a subject of a real investigation, meaning one that may lead to criminal charges, unless there is a grand jury. That's not going to happen until the Justice Department comes on board. The Obama administration's window dressing is letting the FBI investigate without Justice Department prosecutors and the grand jury. The question remains as to how far Obama will keep be willing to stick his neck out for Hillary Clinton in her presidential bid. It's all rotten to the core.

89. Former President Bill Clinton, politicking on behalf of his wife in Washington state on Monday, March 21, 2016, urged people to vote for Hillary "if you believe we've finally come to the point where we can put the awful legacy of the last eight years behind us." *What?* Is damage control needed? Isn't Obama a Democrat? Isn't Hillary a Democrat? That's what Bill said about the awful legacy, and it seems reasonable to understand that he and Hillary are fed up with Obama's eight years in the White House. Maybe Bill Clinton was referring to something else, maybe not. Hillary Clinton was a part of that awful legacy while serving as secretary of state. Bill obviously doesn't want that awful legacy to continue.

90. Environmentalists distrust Hillary Clinton because climate change has not really been her issue. It's a late add-on to the Hillary camp of perceived knowledge and only a topic. Vulnerable communities are being hit the hardest. As an example: it's pretty alarming if the asthma rates in the United States are superimposed over a map of where coal plants are. Her campaign rhetoric claims she wants the United States to be the clean energy superpower of the twenty-first century. By the end of her first presidential term, she wants 500 million solar panels installed. She wants the United States to generate enough clean energy to power all homes in the next ten years. It certainly sounds like she's blowing a lot of campaign hot air to get votes. *500 million?*

91. Hillary Clinton took the Obama administration's affection for fracking and set up a whole office at the State Department to push it all over the world. Fracking refers to the procedure of creating fractures in rock formations by injecting fluid into cracks to force them further open. That allows more extractable oil and gas to flow out of the formation. Studies strongly indicate that fracking is bad for infant health including the possibility that infants are being harmed by air pollution associated with fracking activity. Thus the demand for cheap energy could be doing irreversible harm to children. That's reason enough for serious pause and for Hillary to delay her fracking efforts. She is not.

92. Hillary Clinton is full of failed ideas and plans to combat terrorism. In her speech on the topic in the wake of the attacks in Brussels (March 2016), she blasted the Republican candidates for condoning torture as a means of fighting terrorists. Republican Donald Trump was quick to respond to Clinton's remarks in his tweet, "Just watched Hillary deliver a pre-packaged speech on terror. She's been in office fighting terror for 20 years—and look where we are!" Trump also branded Clinton as incompetent, questioning his rival's capability to be commander-in-chief. "She doesn't have a clue. She's made such bad decisions."

93. Massachusetts state law forbids electioneering and campaigning for, or against a candidate within 150 feet of a polling location. Not applicable for Bill as a "Clinton Privilege" of being above the law was put into play during several Massachusetts polling locations on Super Tuesday, March 01, 2016. Voters were disrupted by the extra security and bottlenecks, as many had gotten off work to vote and became frustrated with the unnecessary delays and commotion created by Bill Clinton's political visits. The "Clinton Privilege" became so rampant at one location that Bernie Sanders backers were ordered to campaign further away, while Bill was handed a bullhorn to campaign the crowd for Hillary within earshot of the polling place's door. It was just another prime example of the abusive-use-of-power tactic to be expected if Hillary gets into the White House.

94. From WikiLeaks documents: Hillary Clinton's abusive-use-of-power tactics ordered diplomats to spy on UN leaders. Those were clear violations of international law. A classified directive signed by Secretary of State Clinton (2009) ordered US diplomats to spy on the highest-ranking officials in the United Nations. The targets included UN Secretary General Ban Ki Moon and ambassadors of the permanent members of the UN Security Council—China, France, Russia, and the UK. The UN has previously asserted that bugging the secretary general was illegal, citing the 1946 UN convention on privileges and immunities, and the 1961 Vienna convention, among others.

95. Hillary Clinton has a pattern of secrecy and receiving unethical transgressions (money) going back several years. There was a 2008 CNN piece entitled, "Obama camp slams Clinton for secrecy" in which Obama strategist David Axelrod said she was the least-vetted candidate in the presidential field because of her refusal to disclose documents (referring to tax returns). Obama's campaign manager, David Plouffe, noted, "Considering the huge amounts of money they (the Clintons) have made in recent years, they've contributed their money to the campaign, some of those relationships financially have been with individuals who have come under quite a bit of scrutiny for possible ethics transgressions, it's essential to the American people to know where they are getting their money from."

96. Her campaign rhetoric often says she wants the rich to pay their "fair share" of taxes. "Fair share" means more. From the Tax Policy Center: Analyzing the bevy of tax proposals she's putting forth would certainly raise the tax burden of the country's highest earners. It may also discourage their incentives to work, save, and invest. Without that, America may take one step forward and two steps backward. The negative impact of Hillary's "fair share" thinking directly increases the incentives for the rich to invest and support any growth of America's economy.

97. Hillary's aide, advisor, and longtime assistant at the State Department, Huma Abedin, was given a special arrangement that allowed her to earn money while serving in a role with the Clinton Foundation at the time she was also a federal employee. The arrangement, and the $135,000 she earned from it, was not disclosed on the State Department's financial forms. That was in violation of a law mandating that public officials must reveal significant sources of income. Hillary Clinton signed off on the special conspiratorial employment deal in March 2012. Huma Abedin's husband is Anthony Weiner, who left Congress amid personal scandal in June 2011, and she is the daughter of Saleha Mahmood Abedin, a pro-Sharia sociologist with ties to numerous Islamist organizations including the Muslim Brotherhood.

98. In 2013 the American public learned that President Obama used the Internal Revenue Service to harass his political opposition. Expect more of the same with Hillary Clinton. The compulsion to decree to one's neighbor what's best for him, while using the federal government to enforce it, is an abrasive abuse of power and affliction. Leading up to the 2012 presidential election, the IRS targeted and singled out conservative groups regarded as enemies of the president. Hillary Clinton, if elected, would rely on the same kind of people to fill the federal bureaucracies. They would be eager with meaningful attempts to impose rules and regulations on the American people that would never fly in Congress. Some of those rules and regulations would get through.

99. What is the case for Hillary? (*Harper's* magazine article 2014): It boils down to this: She has experience, she's a woman, and it's her turn. It's hard to find any substantive political argument in her favor. So the highlight of the article is that Hillary Clinton only has three things going for her—her experience, being a woman, and it's her turn. That's not enough substance in a candidate to be the next president. She's better off speaking and commanding outlandish fees. Politicians who promise they can deliver change while also taking the money mostly just end up taking the money.

100. If Hillary is elected president, she will have four years in which to nominate justices to the Supreme Court. There is already one on deck and no one believes Hillary will choose a moderate. If she's in charge, the next justice could be someone like Senator Al Franken! Even worse, Hillary Clinton is open to the idea of nominating Barack Obama to the US Supreme Court. She's on record as saying, "That's a great idea. He's brilliant and he can set forth an argument and he was a law professor. He's got all the credentials."

101. This reason is certainly from the truth-is-stranger-than-fiction file. In April 2015 Larry Darrell Upright, 81, died at a hospital in Concord, North Carolina. His obituary posted on the Whitley's Funeral Home's website, Kannapolis, North Carolina described him as the father of two and grandfather of three, an avid golfer whose greatest joy was his family. In lieu of flowers, memorials may be sent to Shriners Hospital for Children at 2900 Rocky Point Drive, Tampa, FL 33607. Pretty standard and reverent notations until the last sentence that read, "Also, the family respectfully asks that you do not vote for Hillary Clinton in 2016. R.I.P. Grandaddy." That respectful and sincere request generated hundreds of condolences and comments against Hillary Clinton.

The reasons are numbered 1–101, but in no particular order as to priority. It's up to you, the reader, to pick out your favorites. Decide on your personal TOP TEN reasons and list them! Have fun comparing with friends and family! See how many you agree on.

Want more? Create a list of additional reasons why Hillary should never get anywhere near the White House ever again!

Name: _____

Date: _____

My Top 10 Reasons

Ref.
in Book

#1 _____   _____

#2 _____   _____

#3 _____   _____

#4 _____   _____

#5 _____   _____

#6 _____   _____

#7 _____   _____

#8 _____   _____

#9 _____   _____

#10 _____   _____

Foreign Policy Reasons

#1 _____ _____

#2 _____ _____

#3 _____ _____

#4 _____ _____

#5 _____ _____

#6 _____ _____

#7 _____ _____

#8 _____ _____

#9 _____ _____

#10_____ _____

National Security Policy Reasons

#1 _____ _____

#2 _____ _____

#3 _____ _____

#4 _____ _____

#5 _____ _____

#6 _____ _____

#7 _____ _____

#8 _____ _____

#9 _____ _____

#10 _____ _____

Social Policy Reasons

#1 _____   _____

#2 _____   _____

#3 _____   _____

#4 _____   _____

#5 _____   _____

#6 _____   _____

#7 _____   _____

#8 _____   _____

#9 _____   _____

#10 _____   _____

Health Care Policy Reasons

#1 _____ _____

#2 _____ _____

#3 _____ _____

#4 _____ _____

#5 _____ _____

#6 _____ _____

#7 _____ _____

#8 _____ _____

#9 _____ _____

#10 _____ _____

Economic Policy Reasons

#1 _____   _____

#2 _____   _____

#3 _____   _____

#4 _____   _____

#5 _____   _____

#6 _____   _____

#7 _____   _____

#8 _____   _____

#9 _____   _____

#10 _____   _____

Supreme Court Reasons

#1 _____ _____

#2 _____ _____

#3 _____ _____

#4 _____ _____

#5 _____ _____

#6 _____ _____

#7 _____ _____

#8 _____ _____

#9 _____ _____

#10 _____ _____

Gun Control Policy Reasons

#1 _____   _____

#2 _____   _____

#3 _____   _____

#4 _____   _____

#5 _____   _____

#6 _____   _____

#7 _____   _____

#8 _____   _____

#9 _____   _____

#10 _____   _____

Abortion Policy Reasons

#1 _____ _____

#2 _____ _____

#3 _____ _____

#4 _____ _____

#5 _____ _____

#6 _____ _____

#7 _____ _____

#8 _____ _____

#9 _____ _____

#10 _____ _____

Notes

Notes

Notes

Acknowledgments

Whenever there is a roll call of ones who made this work possible, there are always ones who are inadvertently left out. I apologize for that and will always cherish their hospitality, wise counsel, and friendship. But to the ones listed and to any left out, I can only reciprocate but never repay. However, I do wish to sincerely thank certain persons and all the various press mediums whose unsung contributions to my work were very specific.

Hillary Clinton: A historical lady of the United States

Rita Rosenkranz: Literary agent and business partner

Dr. Deno Trakas: Writing mentor and friend

Krishan Trotman: Initial Skyhorse Publishing editor on project

And to any/all others inadvertently omitted, a sincere thanks.